Divine Election
and
Human Responsibility

by
CORNELIUS R. STAM

Divine Election
and
Human Responsibility

by
CORNELIUS R. STAM

Founder of the Berean Bible Society

BEREAN BIBLE SOCIETY
7609 W. Belmont Ave.
Chicago, Illinois 60635

Copyright, 1994

by

BEREAN LITERATURE FOUNDATION
7609 W. Belmont Avenue
Chicago, Illinois 60635

PRINTED IN U.S.A.

WORZALLA PUBLISHING CO.
STEVENS POINT, WISCONSIN

CONTENTS   Page

Preface 7

CHAPTER I

Divine Election and Human Responsibility: When Heaven and Earth Meet Together—The Lord Jesus Christ—The Bible—Personal Salvation 11

CHAPTER II

Calvinism and Arminianism: The Doctrine of Election—Election and Foreknowledge 18

CHAPTER III

The Doctrine of Limited Redemption —Is It Scriptural? Related Subjects Briefly Considered: Jacob Loved, Esau Hated—God Loves You—"The Whole World"—How Can the Dead Believe? —Faith the Gift of God—Irresistible Grace .. 26

CHAPTER IV

Is the Doctrine of Limited Redemption True Calvinism? (Calvin's Own Testimony)—(Excerpts from His Commentaries and Harmonies) 42

CHAPTER V

A Personal Letter On the Writings of Arthur W. Pink: Further Consideration—Christ's Death for All the Only Legitimate Basis for the Gospel of the Grace of God—If Christ Did Not Die For All, How Do You Know He Died For *You*?— Christ Died For Me—Christ Died For You 46

CHAPTER VI

Can "All Men" Mean All *Kinds* of Men? (A Study of I Timothy 2:1-7)—Let's Think This Through—A Further Thought for Consideration 71

CHAPTER VII

All This To Maintain A Position: 82

CHAPTER VIII

Twenty Problems for Limited Redemptionists To Solve: 86

APPENDIX—A Touching Letter from a Reader 93

PREFACE

It appears that this will be the last of my library size books to come off the press. At age 84 my strength is greatly diminished and my physical faculties less keen. My sight, especially, fails me, often when most urgently needed. Yet, by God's grace, I have finished this volume on election, titled, *Divine Election and Human Responsibility*.

Actually, however, this book is the work of *two* persons: (1)—Pastor Stam and (2)—"our beloved brother Paul." I wrote it; he read it!

This is so in more than one way. Paul Sadler well understands this writer's convictions on election, and holds these convictions as firmly. It was a great encouragement to the author, therefore, to have Pastor Sadler carefully examine this entire volume for sense and sequence and to ask questions and make suggestions along the way.

Heartfelt thanks to Brother Paul. It was a big job and a great help to have my colleague in the ministry do this impor-

ELECTION

tant part of the work, especially in view of my serious sight problem. I cannot see well enough to read even the larger typefaces in this book on Election.

The contents of this book were written in the early 1940's when the battle over divine election was raging.

You will find nothing of this in the *Searchlight* covering the same years, however, for the great contest over dispensational truth was then also being waged, and we did not want to divert our readers' attention away from this. We simply referred inquirers to the proper books.

Paul's unique apostleship, our God-given commission, the "one body," our "all spiritual blessings in heavenly places in Christ," the ministry of the twelve compared with that of Paul—all this and much more, so vital to the dispensation of the grace of God, was being widely discussed, and it was important that these truths remain in the forefront.

Because so many were then embroiled in extreme views on election, and even promoted the teaching of limited redemption—asking us questions about these problems, we submitted our answers in a mimeographed (later offset) packet, now rearranged somewhat and presented to our readers in this book.

This packet, then sent out by the hundreds, was greatly used of God for the salvation of souls—just because the subject matter had so directly to do with salvation.

One whole family of five came to know the Lord Jesus Christ through reading this packet and wrote us a glowing letter of thanks.

We pray that with the subject of divine election again on the rise, this book may likewise be used for the salvation of many, as well as for a clearer understanding of the doctrine of *Divine Election and Human Responsibility.*

Chapter I

Divine Election
and
Human Responsibility

It is an interesting fact that the three great points of contact between God and man are shrouded in mystery. We refer to the Lord Jesus Christ, the Bible and redemption, in each of which God and man, the Infinite and the finite, are joined together.

WHEN HEAVEN AND EARTH MEET TOGETHER

In the teachings of the Word of God as to all three of these subjects, declarations are made which are paradoxical, even antinomian; i.e., apparent contradictions, yet both true to fact. Thus it is our purpose in this volume to induce the reader to simply *believe what God has said,* even when He makes *two* statements which seem logically to contradict each other, remembering that while our poor intellects cannot yet reconcile such statements it does not follow from this that they are indeed irreconcilable.

Take, for example, the person of

THE LORD JESUS CHRIST

Some suppose that Christ was *only* a *man,* but *they are wrong.*

The whole "Gospel According to John" was written to prove that our Lord was—and is—*God,* and His deity is insisted upon in many individual passages of Scripture (Matt. 1:23; John 1:1-5; 8:58; 20:28; Tit. 2:13; Heb. 1:8,10; *et al*).

Others suppose that Christ is *only God,* but *they too are wrong.*

The "Gospel According to Luke" was written to prove that He was—and is—true *Man,* and His humanity is likewise insisted upon in many individual passages of Scripture (Matt. 20:28; Luke 2:11; John 1:14; Gal. 4:4; I Tim. 2:5; I John 4:2,3; II John 7; *et al*).

Still others hold that our Lord was *partly* God and *partly* man, but *they too are wrong.*

For one thing, if He were but *"partly* God" He would not be *God* at all, for in the nature of the case there can be no such thing as a non-infinite *God!*

Divine Election and Human Responsibility

The Bible teaches that our Lord is *wholly* God, and at the same time *wholly* man (though without sin). We are doubtless unable to comprehend this at present, but it is a Scriptural *fact* and to hold any of the other three positions one must ignore plain passages of Scripture or bend them to conform to his own doctrinal views.

Do we thus place God and man on the same level? In no wise, for our Lord's humanity was always subordinate to His deity, yet it remains a *fact* that He *was* both wholly God *and* wholly Man.

THE BIBLE

As with Christ, the living Word, so it is with the Bible, the written Word.

Some hold that it was written *only* by *man,* but *they are wrong.* Everywhere this Book abounds with evidence that *God* was the Author. Its fulfilled prophecies, its sublime harmony, its power to regenerate and transform lives, the authority with which it speaks, never deigning to defend its divine authorship, but rather *assuming* it—all this stamps it as the Book of God. And in addition its divine authorship is declared in many individual passages (Rom. 3:1,2; Eph. 6:17; II Tim. 3:16; Heb. 4:12; 5:12; II Pet. 1:21).

Others hold that the Bible is *only* the Word of *God,* but *these too are wrong.*

It is significant that God chose *Matthew,* the publican, to portray Christ as *King;* Luke, the physician, to portray Him as *Man;* Mark to present Him as *Servant* and John as *God.* These men, individually, were the very ones to present Him as they did. Often, this human authorship is shown to be important. Our Lord frequently reminded His hearers of what *Moses* had said to them in the Scriptures (Matt. 19:8; *et al*). Luke says, "I had a complete understanding of these things from the beginning" (Luke 1:3), implying that he was *qualified* to write about our Lord's earthly ministry. Paul says, "Behold, I Paul say unto you. . ." (Gal. 5:2) implying that *his* saying it should bear weight with his readers. The freedom with which many of these men wrote is manifest in many passages, as for example the closing paragraphs of Paul's epistles where he sends greetings to individuals, asks for the cloak he had left at Troas, etc. Surely he had no idea at the time that he was writing the Word of God.

To solve this problem still others have concluded that the Bible is *partly* the Word of God and *partly* the word of man, but *these too are wrong*. If they were right we would still be without an authoritative revelation from God, for none of us could ascertain with certainty what was written by man and what by God.

The truth is that the Bible is *wholly* the Word of God, yet at the same time, *wholly* the word of man, and to hold any of the other three positions one must ignore plain passages of Scripture or bend them to conform to his own doctrinal views. It is the miracle of divine inspiration that a man could sit down and write, in one mood or another, with complete freedom to express himself and lo, what he writes is also, every word, the Word of God! We cannot comprehend this, but the regenerate heart bows in faith to the Word and says: "I believe."

Do we then place God and man on the

same level? By no means, for the human writers in every case were subordinate to the divine Author. Yet it remains a *fact* that the Bible *was* written *wholly* by man and at the same time *wholly* by God.

PERSONAL SALVATION

Now let us apply the same principle to the subject of personal salvation. Generalizing for the moment, we may correctly state:

Some hold that salvation is dependent *only* on the will of man. *They are wrong,* for the Scriptures indicate all too clearly that *"salvation is of the Lord."*

Others hold that salvation is dependent *only* on the will of God. *These too are wrong,* for the Scriptures also teach that men who do not desire to be saved are not saved and *cannot* justly be saved.

Still others seek to solve the problem by rationalizing that salvation is *partly* dependent upon God's will and *partly* on man's; that God has an over-all plan, but that man fills in the details, so to speak. *These too are wrong* as we shall see.

The truth is that salvation depends

wholly upon the will of God and also *wholly* upon the will of man. God must *will* a man to be saved if he is to be saved at all, yet that man must also exercise *his will* as a responsible moral agent if he is to be saved. He must *will* to be saved. Rom. 9:16, of course, teaches simply that it is God whose will is first exercised, and operates upon man's will. We are doubtless unable at present to reconcile the doctrine of divine election with that of human responsibility, but both are declared to be true and to take any of the other three positions one must ignore or alter plain passages of Scripture. We must bow in faith and believe *both* doctrines.

Do we then place God and man on the same level by holding the above view? No indeed, for we confess that man's will is subordinate to God's, yet it remains a Scriptural *fact* that salvation is *wholly* by the will of God (this is grace), yet also *wholly* by the will of *man* (this is faith).

Chapter II
Calvinism and Arminianism

Does it not appear that largely Calvinists and Arminians are right in what they affirm, but wrong in what they deny; that each departed from the Scriptures in seeking to maintain their position by attempts to *explain away* the Scriptural arguments of the other?

The Calvinists *proved* the doctrine of God's sovereign grace in election, but they went astray in trying to *dis*prove man's freedom of choice (qualified by his depraved condition) and his moral responsibility.

Similarly, the Arminians *proved* their doctrines of responsible moral agency, but departed from Scripture in their attempts to *dis*prove God's sovereign grace in election.

Also, it may have been rightly said that "Both are right in principle, but, in varying degrees, wrong through one-sided over-emphasis."

√ Finally: It is not ours to reconcile in

our minds God's love to all with His sovereignty in election, or His supernatural saving work with His wrath against those who do not receive His grace, or His complete sovereignty in salvation with man's responsibility to receive it. It is ours only to bow before all that Scripture has said and to humbly respond: *"I believe."*

In this particular matter the true preacher is *both* a Presbyterian and a Methodist. Before the service he prays: "Lord, work in their hearts. If Thou dost not work none will be saved." Yet half an hour later he is saying to the congregation: "You are responsible to choose. Believe and you will be saved; reject and the wrath of God will abide upon you." In *both* attitudes this preacher is Scriptural, and only in this way can he experience the power of God in his ministry.

As a simple illustration we might depict a young man with an electric motor and a "plugged in" wire in his hands. An electrician advises him: "Attach the wire to the motor and it will run." The young man notices, though, that the wire is really *two* wires (one positive and the other negative). Assuming he should attach the positive one he tries this but the motor will not run. Concluding he was wrong about this he then attaches the negative one, also in vain. The electrician then tells him to attach them *both*. "But how can the motor possibly run then," the young man asks; "One is positive and the other negative?" "Nevertheless attach them both," replies the electrician. So the young man attaches them both and, lo, the motor runs!

So we are required as believers in the Word of God to believe two doctrines which we cannot as yet reconcile. If, to maintain our "consistency" we rationalize one or the other away, we dishonor God and rob ourselves of the power of the Spirit.

In the words of Sir Robert Anderson: "To say these doctrines *seem* incompatible may be permitted, but to say they *are* incompatible is to exalt human reason above divine revelation" and Paul exhorts us: *"learn in us not to think above that which is written."*

We close by quoting from Dr. Chafer's *Systematic Theology,* Vol. III, p. 184:

"The disagreement now under discussion is not between orthodox and heterodox men; it is within the fellowship of those who have most in common and who need the support and encouragement of each other's confidence. Few themes have drawn out more sincere and scholarly investigation."

THE DOCTRINE OF ELECTION

The Arminian view of election is not election at all. According to this school of thought "common grace" provides all sinners with the ability to turn in faith to Christ. Election is thus made to be dependent upon foreseen human faith, and is the consequent recognition of that faith.

Consistently Arminians teach that therefore man must continue in faith (and its fruits) to remain saved.

This doctrine does violence to a whole volume of important passages of Scripture, some of which we quote here:

ELECTION

"There is *none* that seeketh after God" (Rom. 3:11).

"No man can come to Me, *except the Father which hath sent Me draw him*" (John 6:44).

". . . God hath from the beginning *chosen you to salvation* through sanctification of the Spirit and belief of the truth" (II Thes. 2:13).

"According as He hath *chosen* us in Him *before the foundation of the world,* that we should be holy and without blame before Him,

"In love having *predestinated* us unto the adoption of children [sons] . . .

"To the praise of the glory of His grace, wherein He hath made us accepted in the Beloved. . . .

"In whom also we have obtained an inheritance, being predestinated according to the purpose of Him who worketh all things after the counsel of His own will:

"That we should be to the praise of *His glory,* who first trusted in Christ" (Eph. 1:4-6,11,12).

Thus believers are said to be *"God's elect"* (Rom. 8:33), *"the called according to His purpose"* (Rom. 8:28), "vessels of mercy . . . *afore prepared unto glory"* (Rom. 9:23), *"chosen in the Lord"* (Rom. 16:13), etc.

The doctrine of election, rightly taught, should not discourage, but rather encourage the fearful sinner. We have seen from II Thes. 2:13 that election and faith are inseparably connected. Thus the anxious sinner may be assured that since *some* will be saved and salvation is received by faith, *he* will be saved if he believes.

Or, to put it in another way, is a sinner anxious that he may not be among the elect? Then let him call upon God to save him through Christ and see if he is rejected! Rom. 10:13 assures him that he will be saved.

ELECTION AND FOREKNOWLEDGE

In Rom. 8:29 the Apostle Paul declares of God that "whom He did *foreknow,* he *also* did predestinate. . ." and in I Pet. 1:2 believers are said to be "elect *according to the foreknowledge of God."*

We have already dealt with the Arminian view of God's foreknowledge, which represents it as merely knowing beforehand who will believe and be saved. This view is completely unacceptable since the saved are said to have been *"chosen"* in Christ *"before the foundation of the world"* (Eph. 1:4).

But neither can we accept the view which makes God's foreknowledge "that which He purposes to bring to pass" (Dr. Lewis Sperry Chafer in *Systematic Theology,* Vol. VII, P. 158). If God's foreknowledge *is* His eternal purpose, then words have no meaning. *Foreknowledge* and *election* are *not* the same thing!

If Rom. 8:29 and I Pet. 1:2 mean anything they mean that election and predestination are *based upon* the foreknowledge of God. Therefore it is our belief that these passages refer to God's foreknowledge of *all things*—of all involved in the salvation of any sinner. Why limit the foreknowledge of *God* to His merely knowing who will be saved, on the one hand, or to His *purpose* in election on the other? Surely *God* does know *all* things, thus, highly as we respect the late Dr. Chafer, we must take issue with his stated view that God's foreknowledge should be "distinguished from" His omniscience *(Ibid).*

Salvation is the result of God's *love* to sinners. Therefore the Scriptures would teach us that He did not elect some *arbitrarily,* and pass others by, without regard to principle, but only on the ground of volition or caprice. Rather, knowing all things (as no judge on earth ever can) He could and did elect justly. We may not *now* understand why He elected some and passed others by, and we know assuredly that *none* of us deserved to be elected, but one day we shall fully understand the truth of the Scripture: *"Shall not the Judge of all the earth do right?"*

Chapter III

The Doctrine of Limited Redemption—Is It Scriptural?

Some have concluded from what the Bible says about election that God loved *only* the elect and that Christ died for *only* the elect. Such, however, have adopted this view as a "logical" conclusion, utterly without Scriptural foundation, for *there is no passage of Scripture which says that Christ died for the elect alone.*

One brother has written: *"Paul never writes that God loved the world."* But what does this prove? *Our Lord did* say that God loves the world and in this matter dispensationalism is no factor. Paul *does* declare again and again that God loved, and Christ died for, *"all men," "every man,"* etc.

Others cite passages where it is stated that God loved, or Christ died for, the saved, as for example, Rom. 5:8: "Christ died *for us.*" One friend has sent us what he calls an "impressive list" of such pas-

*The Doctrine of Limited Redemption
Is It Scriptural?*

sages. But neither this nor any comparable passage indicates that Christ died *only* "for us." If it did we might also argue that Christ died for Paul alone, for in Gal. 2:20 he says: "He gave Himself for *me.*"

If our Lord did not die for the non-elect, how can they be condemned for not believing in Him as Savior? (See John 3:18; 16:8,9).

Limited Redemptionists usually interpret the word "world" in John 3:16 and similar passages to refer to "the world of the elect." In the first place, this is a strained and unnatural interpretation, but in the second, our Lord consistently *distinguished* His own from the "world" (same original word). (See John 15:18, 19; 17:15; I John 5:19).

Furthermore, as the gospel (good news) of the kingdom was sent to "all nations," "all the world" and "every creature," so the gospel of God's reconciling grace is "for all" and the Apostle Paul pleads with all: "Be ye reconciled to God," on the basis of the fact that God has made Christ "to be sin for us" (II Cor. 5:14-21). How could Paul, or how can any evangelist plead with men in general to be reconciled on this basis, if Christ did *not* die for all? Or how could any of the apostles proclaim "good news" to all if there is *no good news* for some?

We believe in the doctrine of divine election and will not erase from the Bible such passages as Eph. 1:1-11, but we also believe in the doctrine of God's love to all men and of man's consequent responsibility to accept what that love provides. Hence we likewise refuse to erase from the Bible such passages as I Tim. 2:1-7.

We hold that of those who have not been *already convinced of* "Limited Love" and "Limited Redemption," one hundred out of one hundred will conclude from the following Scripture passages that God loves and that Christ died for *"the world," "the whole world," "all men," "every man."* To make the following passages mean anything else one would have to explain *away* their obvious meaning. Perhaps it will do the reader good to read *all* these Scripture passages through first (left hand column) and then our comments at the right.

The Doctrine of Limited Redemption Is It Scriptural?

Ezek. 33:11: "... as I live, saith the Lord God, I HAVE NO PLEASURE IN THE DEATH OF THE WICKED; BUT THAT THE WICKED TURN FROM HIS WAY AND LIVE...."	Are "the wicked" here the elect? God says in this passage that He desires that they live. This is a refutation of the doctrine of "Limited Redemption."
John 3:16,17: "For God so loved THE WORLD, that He gave His only begotten Son, that WHOSOEVER believeth in Him should not perish, but have everlasting life. "For God SENT NOT HIS SON INTO THE WORLD TO CONDEMN THE WORLD; BUT THAT THE WORLD THROUGH HIM MIGHT BE SAVED."	Clearly, the "world" of 17a is the world of sinners, for *obviously* He did not come to condemn the elect! If the meaning is "God so loved the elect," why doesn't it say so, and why, then, the "whosoever"?
Rom. 3:22: "Even the righteousness of God, which is by faith of Jesus Christ, UNTO ALL and upon all them that believe: for there is no difference."	Since he introduces a *qualification* in the second clause: "and *upon* all them *that believe,"* is it not evident that the phrase "unto all" is *un*qualified; that righteousness is *provided* for *all?*
Rom. 5:18: "Therefore as by the offence of one judgment came upon all men to condemnation; EVEN SO, by the righteousness of One THE FREE GIFT CAME UPON ALL MEN UNTO JUSTIFICATION OF LIFE."	If the first "all men" must be taken *as written,* must not the second "all men" be thus taken? I.e., "the free gift" is to "all men." Note the *"even so."*
Rom. 11:32: "For God hath concluded them all in unbelief, THAT HE MIGHT HAVE MERCY UPON ALL."	Is it not true that only a small part of those whom He concluded in unbelief, and upon whom He had mercy, have indeed believed? So it is mercy *"proffered* to *all."* Note: *"that He might."*

ELECTION

II Cor. 5:14,15: "For the love of Christ constraineth us; because we thus judge, that if ONE DIED FOR ALL, then were all dead: "And that HE DIED FOR ALL, that they which live should not henceforth live unto themselves, but unto Him which died for them and rose again."	He does not say, "He died for all that all might live unto Him." This would be consistent only if the "all" here referred only to the elect. As it is, He died for *all, some* of whom live, and are obligated to "live unto Him."
I Tim. 2:4-6: "WHO WILL HAVE ALL MEN TO BE SAVED, and to come unto the knowledge of the truth. "For there is one God, and ONE MEDIATOR BETWEEN GOD AND MEN, the Man Christ Jesus;"	If the "all men" in Ver. 4 means all the elect, why does Ver. 5 say that Christ is Mediator between God and *"men,"* not *"some* men." And why does it say that Christ "gave Himself a ransom for *all"?* Even Calvin acknowledges here: "He demonstrates that God has at heart the salvation of all, because he invites all to the acknowledgment of the truth."
I Tim. 4:10: ". . . WHO IS THE SAVIOR OF ALL MEN, specially of those that believe."	Another *qualified* statement against the background of an *unqualified* one. If the "all men" are the elect, then who are "those that believe"?
Heb. 2:9: ". . . that He by the grace of God SHOULD TASTE DEATH FOR EVERY MAN."	How could *"every man"* refer to the elect only?
II Pet. 2:1: "...false prophets...false teachers ...who privily shall bring in damnable heresies, denying even THE LORD THAT BOUGHT THEM."	Here it is clearly stated of even false prophets and teachers, that "the Lord . . . *bought them."*

The Doctrine of Limited Redemption Is It Scriptural?

II Pet. 3:9: "The Lord . . . is longsuffering to us-ward, NOT WILLING THAT ANY SHOULD PERISH, BUT THAT ALL SHOULD COME TO REPENTANCE."	Is God waiting lest any of the *elect PERISH?!!* Obviously He is waiting to give *all* an opportunity "to come to repentance."
I John 2:2: "And He is the propitiation for our sins: and not for ours only, but ALSO FOR THE SINS OF THE WHOLE WORLD."	Can it be denied that the word, "our," refers to the elect, or that the "also" refers to the rest of mankind, Christ having died for *"the whole world"*?
Matt. 23:37: "O Jerusalem, Jerusalem . . . how often would I have gathered thy children together, even as a hen gathereth her chickens under her wings, and *ye would not!"*	Does this not clearly indicate that our Lord loved even those who did *not* believe in Him? Further, if they were *not able* to believe why did He say: "I would . . . but *ye would not?"*
II Thes. 2:10: "And with all deceivableness of unrighteousness in THEM THAT PERISH; BECAUSE THEY RECEIVED NOT THE LOVE OF THE TRUTH, THAT THEY MIGHT BE SAVED."	This passage does *not* say that the unbelievers will perish because they were not elected, but *"because they received not the love of the truth, that they might be saved."* How could they be blamed for not believing if they had no power to believe?

In the light of all the above, HOW CAN IT BE DENIED (1) That God *desires* that *all* the wicked turn and live, having *no pleasure* in their death? (2) That God loves the world of sinners, and gave His Son "that WHOSOEVER believeth in Him should not perish but have everlasting life"? (3) That God's righteousness is *proffered* to all men, and *conferred* "upon" all those who believe? (4) That "the free gift" is offered "to *all men,* unto justification of life"? (5) That God concluded "all" in unbelief, that He might have mercy upon "all"? (6) That *in addition* to "those who live," Christ died for others: "all"? (7) That God desires that *all* men be saved, that Christ is the Mediator "between God and *men,* (not "some men,") and that He "gave Himself a ransom for *all* [men]"? (8) That He is the Savior (potentially) of *"all men,"* but "specially" (actually) of those who believe? (9) That our Lord "TASTED DEATH *FOR EVERY MAN,"* (10) even for false prophets and teachers whom He "bought" with His blood? (11) That God does not desire "that *any* should perish but that *all* should come to repentance"? (12) That Christ is the satisfaction for the sins of the elect, but *"not only"* for theirs: *"also* for the sins of *the whole world"?* (13) That unbelievers are lost even though *God desires to save them?* (14) That God accepts *none* of the responsibility for the unbelief of the lost, but places it entirely upon *them,* since they are condemned and punished for *not believing?* Note the phrase, "love of the truth," i.e., the love which prompted God to offer salvation through Christ—love which unbelievers *reject.*

Is it quite honest of our *Limited Love* and *Limited Redemption* friends to call their doctrine *Calvinism* when Calvin opposed these errors? It was the Dutch theologians who out-Calvined Calvin, yet called themselves *Calvinists,* but by now our Limited Redemption friends should be well aware of these facts. Certainly they do not teach Calvinism.

RELATED SUBJECTS BRIEFLY CONSIDERED

JACOB LOVED, ESAU HATED

Paul's quotation of the statement, *"Jacob have I loved, but Esau have I hated"* (Rom. 9:13), has been used to refute the clear statements of Scripture that God loves all men and desires their salvation. But *this* was not said by God before the two sons were born. At *that* time, as Paul points out in Verses 11,12, He said merely: *"The elder shall serve the younger."* It was Malachi, *long after* Esau had demonstrated his callous unbelief and Jacob his deep desire for God, who was inspired to say: *"Jacob have I loved, but Esau have I hated"* (Mal. 1:2,3). It was only as a blatant unbeliever that God "hated" Esau. Rom. 9:13, erroneously interpreted, is the general mainstay of those who deny that God loves all men and desires their salvation. They teach from this verse that God loves some and hates others—*before they are even born!*

GOD LOVES YOU

If the passages presented in the above list of Scriptures do not mean what they say; if God does not love all men and Christ did not die for all, then the evangelist cannot honestly say to his hearers: "God loves you; Christ died for you." He would have to say: *"Perhaps* God loves *some* of you, *perhaps* Christ died for *some* of you." How contrary this would be to the general teaching of Scripture! Moreover, the greatest motivation to true faith is the Holy Spirit's use of the truth that God *does* love the hearer and that Christ *did* die for him, whomever he may be.

*The Doctrine of Limited Redemption
Is It Scriptural?*

Surely the great appeal of Scriptural evangelism has never been the message that God "hates," or that Christ did *not* die for some, or most, of those in the audience!

"THE WHOLE WORLD"

Where, in Scripture, does it clearly state, or even clearly imply, that the word "world" (Gr. *kosmos*) means only the elect? Who but a theologian, with a theological system to defend, would ever have taken John 3:16 to refer to "the world of the elect"? And who but a theologian, determined to defend his theological position at any cost, would read "the elect" into *"the whole world"* of I John 2:2:

"He is the propitiation for our sins, and not for ours only, but also for the sins of THE WHOLE WORLD."

HOW CAN THE DEAD BELIEVE?

Extreme Calvinists often ask us, with regard to Eph. 2:1: "How can a dead person believe?" We reply: "How can a dead person be disobedient? How can a dead person walk?" We ask this because the very same passage states that those who are "dead in trespasses and sins" *do* "*walk* according to the course of this world" and *are* "disobedient" (Ver. 3). Moreover, Verse 4 goes on to declare that for this God was *angry* with them, and that they were by nature "the children of *wrath.*" Why should God be angry with them if they were dead so that they *could not* believe?

God uses various metaphors and symbols to convey *various aspects of the truth,* but it is always unwise to draw implications from them at random or to apply them indiscriminately.

Obviously God does *not* use the word "dead" in Eph. 2:1 to denote insensibility or cessation of activity, for *these* "dead" *walk* and are *disobedient.* Evidently He uses the word "dead" to show that all human hope is gone. As the body merely goes into corruption at death, so man's spiritual condition is hopeless but for God, "who is rich in mercy," love and power.

FAITH THE GIFT OF GOD

Surely faith *is* the gift of God, but this is not the *whole* story. If Eph. 2:8 means that faith is *directly,* or *only* "the gift of God"; that God directly injects it into the human heart, how shall we account for the following:

"Without faith it is impossible to PLEASE Him, for he that cometh to God, *must believe* that He is, and that He is A REWARDER OF THEM THAT DILIGENTLY SEEK HIM" (Heb. 11:6).

How can I *please God* by believing, if such believing is wholly *His* work and not mine? And why should He *reward MEN* for something which He Himself has wrought in and for them?

Again, if "No man seeketh after God" (so often quoted by extreme Calvinists) is the *whole* truth, why should God "reward" those who "diligently seek Him"? (Cf. here John 3:18,36). But there is more:

Of course faith is, in the broadest sense, like everything we have, a gift of God. Our power to think, to plan, to compare, to decide—and half a dozen other faculties—are all gifts from God. "What have ye that ye did not receive?"

But our Calvinist friends have taken this to mean that in some supernatural way God *implants* or *injects* faith into the hearts of those He has elected to salvation. This is an unscriptural view.

1. Let theologians on both sides of the question argue the grammar of this passage, but there is, I believe, an easier way. Ephesians 2:9 is also part of the sentence. Thus if it is faith that is (in this sense) the gift of God, why should he explain that it is "not of works"? How could faith possibly be of works? or why should the Apostle have to state that faith is not of works; no one thinks it is. The Scriptures present it as the *opposite* of works. But many *do* think that *salvation* is of works; hence his declaration that it is "the *gift* of God, *not of works*...."

2. I know of no passage of Scripture that states that God implants or injects faith into the heart. The nearest might be Acts 16:14, but the Lord opened Lydia's heart *providentially*. She was already a *worshipper of God,* and one of a faithful few who were to be found at the riverside in Philippi, *praying*. And it was to this seeking soul that God sent Paul, who told her truths that she then gladly "attended to."

3. As to Eph. 2:8, where else do we read that *faith* is the gift of God, particularly in the special sense applied to it by

the Calvinists? But I do read again and again that *salvation* is the gift of God (John 4:10; Rom. 5:15-18; 6:23, *et al,* including Eph. 2:8!) Let the reader consult his concordance and see how many passages there are that state or clearly imply that salvation is the *"gift,"* or *"free gift"* of God.

4. The Scriptures do state specifically that "faith *cometh by hearing* and hearing *by the Word of God"* (Rom. 10:17), and that *the Word* is the "incorruptible *seed"* that *begets life* in us (I Pet. 1:23,25). Thus, as the Word (written by the Holy Spirit), convicts the sinner (Is not this the work of the Spirit?) and he receives this "incorruptible seed," "the Word, *which by the gospel is preached unto you,"* imparts eternal life to him.

5. If faith is the gift of God in the sense that He supernaturally *implants* or *injects* it into the hearts of the elect alone, how could God justly hold the non-elect responsible for *not* believing? II Thes. 2:10 seems to suggest this enigma when it says that unbelievers will "perish, because *they* received not *the LOVE of the truth."*

ELECTION

IRRESISTIBLE GRACE

This is a human designation, not a Scriptural one.

God tells man His love story and says: "Believe, and be saved." He condemns those who do not believe, and is angry that they have spurned His love.

If the unqualified doctrine of "irresistible grace" is valid, is not man a mere puppet, manipulated by God? Is not the unqualified doctrine of "irresistible grace" pure fatalism?

Does not the unqualified doctrine of "irresistible grace" negate one precious aspect of grace, i.e., that salvation is offered freely to all (Rom. 10:12,13) without favoritism of any kind? (Cf. Tit. 2:11). In this case, are not the "whosoever" passages a cruel mockery?

Has it ever been an effective or Scriptural way to induce sinners to believe God's message of grace to tell them that they *cannot* believe?

If God bestowed grace in a way that is unqualifiedly "irresistible," would He not be adulterating grace with an element that is *not* grace?

Does not Paul declare that man, even in his fallen state, is still "the image and glory of God" (I Cor. 11:7)? Does this not indicate that he has a certain independence of purpose and will, though his will, indeed, is neither pure nor sovereign?

Chapter IV

Is the Doctrine of Limited Redemption True Calvinism?

(Calvin's Own Testimony)

(Excerpts from His Commentaries and Harmonies)

Matt. 23:37: "The city itself, indeed, over which He had lately wept (Luke 19:41) is still the object of His compassion . . . for not once and again did God wish to gather them together, but, by constant and and uninterrupted advances, had sent to them the prophets, one after another, almost all of whom were rejected by the great body of people. . . . There is an emphatic contrast between God's *willing* and their *not willing* (At Matt. 23:37).

Matt. 26:28: "By the word *many* he means not a part of the world only, but the whole human race" (Harmonies, Vol. III, P. 214).

Mark 14:24: "By the word *many* he means not a part of the world only, but the whole human race" (*Ibid.*).

Is the Doctrine of Limited Redemption True Calvinism?

Luke 22:19: "Therefore, when we approach the holy table, let us not only remember in general that *the world has been redeemed by the blood of Christ,* but let every one consider for himself that his own sins have been expiated" *(Ibid.)*

John 1:29: "He uses the word *sin* in the singular number, for any kind of iniquity; as if he had said, that every kind of unrighteousness which alienates men from God is taken away by Christ. And when he says, the sin OF THE WORLD, he extends this favor indiscriminately to the whole human race" (At John 1:29).

John 3:15,16: ". . . he has employed the universal term *whosoever,* both to invite all indiscriminately to partake of life, and to cut off every excuse for unbelievers. Such is also the import of the term *world* . . . for though nothing will be found in *the world* that is worthy of the favor of God yet he shows himself to be reconciled to the whole world, when he invites all men without exception to the faith of Christ. . ." (At John 3:15,16).

John 3:16: ". . . the Heavenly Father loves the *human race,* and wishes that they should not perish?" (At John 3:16).

John 3:17: "The word *world* is again repeated, that no man may think himself wholly excluded, if he only keep the road of faith" (At John 3:17).

John 12:47: ". . . He delays to pronounce *judgment* on them, because on the contrary, He has come for the salvation of all. . . . He lays aside for a time the office of *judge,* and offers salvation to all without reserve, and stretches out his arms to embrace all, that all may be the more encouraged to repent" (At John 12:47).

John 16:11: "Under the term *world* are, I think, included not only those who would be truly converted to Christ, but hypocrites and reprobates" (At John 16:11).

Rom. 5:18: "He makes this favor common to all, because it is propounded to all, not because it is in reality extended to all [i.e., experientially]; for though Christ suffered for the sins of the whole world, it is offered through God's benignity indiscriminately to all, yet all do not receive him" (At Rom. 5:18).

Rom. 11:32: ". . . this mercy is without

difference offered to all, but every one must seek it by faith" (At Rom. 11:32).

Col. 1:14: "He says that redemption was procured through the blood of Christ, for by the sacrifice of his death all the sins of the world have been expiated" (At Col. 1:14).

I Tim. 2:4-6: ". . . he demonstrates that God has at heart the salvation of all, because he invites all to the acknowledgment of His truth" (At I Tim. 2:4-6).

II Peter 3:9: "So wonderful is his love toward mankind, that he would have them all to be saved" (At II Pet. 3:9).

Chapter V

A Personal Letter On the Writings of Arthur W. Pink

(July, 1975)

Dear Brother:

Sincere thanks for your patience in waiting for my appraisal of Arthur W. Pink's views on election.

If at times I seem harsh with him it will be only to press home a point I feel to be important. Surely there will be nothing personal in it, either toward him or toward anyone else. I know that you will read the following with this in mind.

In considering Mr. Pink's published works we must bear in mind that he was an anti-dispensationalist, who confused "the gospel of the kingdom" with "the gospel of the grace of God" and did not recognize the dispensation of the mystery uniquely committed to Paul. Therefore he *could not,* for example, accept I Timothy 2:4-7 *just as it is written.*

Mr. Pink believed that the Law of the

Sabbath (to him the 1st or any *one* day of the week) is binding upon believers today.

I knew him personally and heard him argue at length for this view in our home and at the church we attended. I have somewhere in my possessions a copy of a reply to Pink's position on this subject by Pastor Edward Drew, then of Paterson, N.J.

I was brought up in a denomination where Limited Love and Limited Redemption were taught just as Mr. Pink has taught them, and I know the despair they caused as serious-minded people asked: "How can I believe that Christ died for *my* sins, when the Bible doesn't say so? How do I know if I am one of the elect?" Thank God, our family was delivered from the shackles of this fearful error and brought into the sunlight of His grace, so that we could then tell men how *"Christ died for all"* and how God *"will have all men to be saved"* (II Cor. 5:14; I Tim. 2:4,6,7).

We readily acknowledge that Mr. Pink has written many good things; so have other anti-dispensationalists. But his legalism, we believe, colored his thinking about God and His grace. Furthermore, his extreme views on election should *not* be considered Calvinism, for they do not accurately represent Calvin's published views any more than do the so-called "Five Points of Calvinism," composed by Dutch theologians after his death.

Please bear in mind that we do *not* deny or question the precious doctrine of divine election. We have consistently and vigorously contended for this blessed truth. But we *do* deny as unscriptural the doctrines of *Limited Love* and *Limited Redemption* which are sometimes attributed to Calvin.

Some time ago I consulted Calvin's Commentaries on the New Testament, with regard to fifteen passages of Scripture which bear upon the question of God's love for all men or/and Christ's death for all. In *every one* of these his commentary emphasizes his belief that they mean exactly what they say: that God *does* love, and that Christ *did* die for *all men,* not merely an elect few. There must be many more such passages in Calvin's voluminous writings.

A Personal Letter On the Writings of Arthur W. Pink

Rather than take many pages to review Mr. Pink's book, *The Sovereignty of God,* we deal here with his 30-page treatment of *The Doctrine of Election,* praying that God will use this to help some who have been influenced by Mr. Pink's writings to see the error of his views *on this subject.*

While we will be forced, by lack of space, to quote some of Mr. Pink's statements *out of* context, we will be careful not to quote them in any way that will change his meaning.

On Page 3 of his booklet Mr. Pink says:

"In short, He [God] is the Decider and Determiner of every man's destiny and the Controller of every detail in each individual's life. . . ."

The first part of this statement, that God is "the Decider and Determiner of every man's destiny" is, to say the very least, a one-sided declaration, which ignores a whole volume of Scripture passages in which God holds *man* responsible for his destiny. We cite only three:

Ezek. 33:11: ". . . as I live, saith the Lord God, I HAVE NO PLEASURE IN THE DEATH OF THE WICKED; but that the wicked turn from his way and live. . . ."

49

John 3:18: "He that believeth on Him is not condemned: but HE THAT BELIEVETH NOT IS *CONDEMNED* ALREADY, *BECAUSE HE HATH NOT BELIEVED* ON THE ONLY BEGOTTEN SON OF GOD."

John 3:36: "He that believeth on the Son hath everlasting life: and HE THAT BELIEVETH NOT THE SON SHALL NOT SEE LIFE, BUT THE *WRATH* OF GOD ABIDETH ON HIM."

But to say that God is "the Controller of every detail in each individual's life" is a still more grievous error, for it makes God the author of sin.

If Pink had said that God *overrules* in every detail we would agree. Even if he had said that God controls the *extent* to which men are permitted to go in their sins, we would not object, but he has said that God is "the *Controller* of *every detail* in each individual's life" (Italics mine).

The Universalists say the same—and argue further that therefore it is only just that God should finally reconcile all to Himself.

Why should the drunkard, the rapist, the murderer be condemned for what he does under God's control?

Here we must pause to insist that

when Pink *also* makes statements that hold man accountable for his sins, he does not thereby justify such statements as the above, or offset their evil effect. Pink has certainly not been consistent in his all-out effort to prove "Limited Love" and "Limited Redemption."

If God is "the Controller of every detail in each individual's life," how can anyone ever be out of the will of God? And what, then, shall we do with such a Scripture passage as Eph. 2:2,3, where *God* says that we were all "the children of *DISOBEDIENCE*," and therefore, by nature "the children of *WRATH*."

If God is "the Controller of every detail in each individual's life," why should He be angry over *anything* man may do, and why should Gen. 6:5,6 declare that:

"God saw that the wickedness of man was great . . . and . . . only evil continually, and it repented the Lord that He had made man on the earth, and IT GRIEVED HIM AT HIS HEART."

Much has been written to explain the meaning of the word "repented" in this passage, but I have never heard Pink's followers explain the words which I have capitalized, words which are obviously important to the meaning of the passage as a whole.

Surely God's heart would not have been grieved if He Himself had been controlling the lives of the wicked antediluvians!

Were the Israelites under God's control when they offered sacrifices to Molech? *He* says that "this abomination" was *contrary* to *His* desire (Jer. 32:35).

Are *we* under God's control when we disobey His will? In such a case we are, to be sure, *subject* to His *overruling* power, but surely we are not being *controlled* by Him. The believers at Pentecost were wholly under God's control because "they were all *filled* with the Holy Spirit." [This is why they could do no wrong during that brief period.] But Pentecost is past and God now controls His saints only in the measure that they yield to the Holy Spirit (Rom. 6:13; 12:1, 2). If God were now "the Controller of every detail in each individual's life," how could we do anything He did not want us to do? How could we be charged with *disobedience?*

Upon this error by Pink is built the further error that God has desired and willed some (the vast majority) to be damned as non-elect. This is in itself a serious error, but the more so in the light of its thrust against the very nature of God.

God's own Word says that *God IS LOVE*. Can it be, then, that He does *not* love the vast majority of mankind? Indeed, the argument that God, from eternity, did not love the non-elect makes of Him a being so hard and cruel that Pink's followers are forever trying to qualify his statements to this effect and to explain away their clear implications.

Believing that God does *not* love the non-elect, some of them will still give a public invitation at the close of the service for the unsaved to receive Christ, or will hold street meetings and plead with men to be saved. How inconsistent!

We have dealt at length with this statement from Pink's *Doctrine of Election* because it lies at the very heart of his unscriptural doctrine of *Limited Love* and *Limited Redemption*. We will now deal more briefly with some of the other errors in this booklet.

Page 5: "Why God selected these particular individuals rather than others, we do not know. His choice is a sovereign one, wholly gratuitous, and dependent upon nothing outside of Himself." How terrible!

There is indeed much that we do not know about election, but is Mr. Pink not at least failing to declare the *whole* truth on this subject when he states that God's choice is *"wholly gratuitous, and dependent upon nothing outside of Himself?"* We press home again the two passages from John's gospel quoted above, as representative of many others:

John 3:18,19: ". . . he that believeth not is condemned." Why? "BECAUSE HE HATH NOT BELIEVED in the only begotten Son of God.

"And THIS IS THE CONDEMNATION, that light is come into the world, and MEN LOVED DARKNESS RATHER THAN LIGHT, because their deeds were evil."

John 3:36: ". . . HE THAT BELIEVETH NOT THE SON shall not see life; but THE *WRATH* OF GOD ABIDETH ON HIM."

*A Personal Letter On the Writings
of Arthur W. Pink*

Does this sound as if men are non-elect wholly and solely because God did not wish them to be saved? And is it not significant that while the Scriptures have so much to say about God's will and purpose to elect some to salvation, they say nothing about any will or purpose to elect the rest to damnation.

Thus, while we agree that we do not know all the reasons why God elected particular individuals rather than others, God's grace in saving *us* must always be a wonder to the believer. We protest against the remainder of Mr. Pink's statement above, in which he implies that *he does* know why: that it was *simply* and *only* because God willed it so.

If "election is a profound mystery," as Pink says on Page 6, why does he then "simplify" it by a declaration that the rejection of the non-elect is *wholly* and *only* God's doing, thus by a wave of the hand contradicting all the plain Scripture passages which insist that this is *not* so?

I have gone to considerable lengths to prove that the three great points of contact between God and man are shrouded in mystery, and if this is so as to the human and divine natures of the Lord Jesus Christ and the human and divine authorship of the Bible, it is no less so of redemption, and an extreme emphasis on God's sovereignty in redemption cannot erase all that God Himself has said about man's responsibility to avail himself of that which God in grace has offered him.

I at least do not say that this great subject is "shrouded in mystery" (as Pink also does), and then turn around and say in effect, "its easy," emphasizing only one line of Scriptures on the subject.

Posing a question which Universalists also ask, Mr. Pink says on Page 7 of his booklet:

"If God can restore to righteousness those who are the willing slaves of sin and have long indulged in the commission of it *without interfering with man's accountability,* why then could He not have *preserved* sinless beings in a state of purity?" (His italics).

But God has *not* restored sinners to righteousness by merely willing it so, or without interfering with man's accountability. Man's accountability *does* enter into the picture, for in grace, and at infinite cost, *Christ* made *Himself* accountable for our sins and settled our debt. Thus we are "justified [declared righteous] freely, by His grace, *through the redemption that is in Christ Jesus*" (Rom. 3:24).

As to why God could not have, or did not, preserve man in a state of purity, Pink's own answer is, "we do not know." But surely our brother should have taken into account the Scriptural declaration that God created man *"in His own image and after His likeness,"* with a mind, a will, power of choice and intelligent purpose. Thus *man* was *responsible to remain obedient to God.*

We have seen that on Pages 3 and 5 of his booklet Mr. Pink states that God is "the Decider and Determiner of every man's destiny" and that "His choice is a sovereign one, *wholly gratuitous and dependent upon nothing outside of Himself.*" But on Pages 7 and 8 he contradicts this by a declaration that differences in men's backgrounds "are among the determining factors of character *and destiny"* (My italics).

Note this carefully, for it shows how weak some of Pink's "strong" statements really are.

If God's choice is "wholly gratuitous [in the sense that it is not called for by circumstances] and dependent upon *nothing outside Himself,* why does Rom. 1:28 state that God gave the Gentiles up because "*they* did not like [wish] to retain *Him* in their knowledge"—and does not this background affect the Gentile world to this day where salvation is concerned? Must we not rather say, where election is concerned: *"Shall not the Judge of all the earth do right?"* (Gen. 18:25, note this entire verse).

On Page 9 of his booklet our brother says:

"The doctrine of Election is clearly taught in God's Word; from cover to cover, the Bible is full of it."

With this, of course, we heartily agree, but farther down the page Mr. Pink again presses this further and makes God to appear arbitrary, peremptory and certainly unjust in electing some and passing others by. Read carefully:

"Esau, the generous-hearted and forgiving spirited, is denied the blessing, though he sought it carefully with tears, while Jacob, the treacherous, underhanded schemer, is fashioned into a vessel of honor" (P. 9).

How unfaithfully, to say the *least,* Pink deals with the record here! Let us see whether *God* depicts Esau and Jacob as Pink has done.

God certainly does *not* portray Esau as the fine character Pink declares him to be. Heb. 12:16 calls him a *"profane person . . . who for one morsel of meat sold his birthright."* Gen. 25:34 says that *"Esau despised his birthright."*

Whereas Mr. Pink calls Esau a "generous-hearted and forgiving spirit," God says: *"And Esau hated Jacob because of the blessing wherewith his father blessed him: and Esau said in his heart . . . I will slay my brother Jacob"* (Gen. 27:41).

As to Jacob, the whole record makes it clear that Jacob, with all his faults, *wanted God,* and therefore the birthright and blessing, and for this God did indeed bless him, for in Heb. 11:20 we are assured that *"by faith* Isaac blessed Jacob and Esau concerning things to come." He learned that Jacob had deceived him but though he *"trembled very exceedingly,"* he saw God's hand in it and said: *"I . . . have blessed him; yea and he shall be blessed"* (Gen. 27:33).

How prone Mr. Pink has been to quote Romans 9:11-13, leaving the impression that God loved Jacob and hated Esau *before they were born,* "that the purpose of God according to election might stand," but *this is not true.* Before they were born, God said of them, *"The elder shall serve the younger"* (Rom. 9:11,12), but it was *long after they had both died* that God said: *"Jacob have I loved, but Esau have I hated"* (Rom. 9:13 cf. Mal. 1:2,3), and this clearly because Jacob *longed for God* while Esau, that "profane person," despised his birthright and the blessing that accompanied it.

Thus it was *after* Esau's flippant rejection of God's blessing and Jacob's earnest desire to have it, that God said: *"Jacob have I loved, but Esau have I hated."*

*A Personal Letter On the Writings
of Arthur W. Pink*

Moreover it was *also after it was too late* that Esau sought the blessing "carefully with tears" (Heb. 11:16,17).

How all these facts of Scripture refute Mr. Pink's portrayal of Esau as a "generous-hearted and forgiving spirited" person, who lost the blessing he so earnestly sought—just because God wanted it so. In other words, whereas Mr. Pink places the responsibility for Esau's rejection upon God (God had planned it so), God places the responsibility squarely upon Esau himself.

On Page 15 our brother says something that is very true, but which contradicts his strong teachings on election:

"Our wisest course is to appeal to His mercy and to His sovereign grace, for there alone is our hope."

Such counsel would come consistently from us, but it is most *in*consistent with *his* view of God's sovereignty.

What will it avail even a sincere person to appeal to God's mercy and grace when even "the generous-hearted and forgiving spirited" Esau was "denied the blessing *though he sought it carefully with tears*"?

61

We point out that he sought it too late, after having *despised* it, but Mr. Pink does not. He says that it was denied to Esau simply because God wanted it so.

On Page 15 again, Mr. Pink says:

"Finally, let it be remembered that God never refuses mercy to those who honestly seek it.

"But if the sinner will not come to Christ that he might have life, then his blood is upon his own head!"

These statements too are most Scriptural but completely <u>inconsistent</u> with his opening declaration that God is "the Decider and Determiner of every man's destiny and *the Controller of every detail in each individual's life"* (Page 3).

All this demonstrates the fact that those who give a one-sided picture of God's sovereignty *cannot* be consistent. If God is the "Controller of every detail in each individual's life," how futile to tell men to seek His mercy! And how unjust to tell them that if they fail to seek it their blood will be on their own heads!

Under his section on "the Difficulties of

Election" Mr. Pink makes up his own convenient list of questions, but does not face up to such basic questions as we have posed, even though these have been asked again and again through past centuries.

We do not question the sovereignty of God or the Scriptural doctrine of election. What we deny is the unscriptural and anti-Pauline argument that God does not love, and that Christ did not die for, *all men.* This Mr. Pink and his followers do not seem to want to face up to. Pink's straightforward way in dodging these issues as if they did not exist is amusing but sad.

Mr. Pink has not recognized the distinctive character of Paul's apostleship and message, but *we do* and therefore we will be the more severely dealt with if we ignore or explain away such clear passages as I Tim. 2:3-7, where we read of *"God our Savior":*

"WHO WILL HAVE *ALL MEN* TO BE SAVED, AND TO COME UNTO THE KNOWLEDGE OF THE TRUTH.

"FOR THERE IS ONE GOD, AND ONE MEDIATOR BETWEEN GOD AND *MEN,* THE MAN CHRIST JESUS;

"WHO GAVE HIMSELF *A RANSOM FOR ALL,* TO BE TESTIFIED IN DUE TIME,

"WHEREUNTO I AM ORDAINED A PREACHER, AND AN APOSTLE, (I SPEAK THE TRUTH IN CHRIST, AND LIE NOT;) A TEACHER OF THE GENTILES IN FAITH AND VERITY."

How could our apostle have stated more clearly that it was given to him to proclaim the blessed truth that it is God's *desire* that all men should be saved? Let's not cast away this blessed aspect of grace and go back into the darkness from which we (certainly I) have been delivered—even though Satan can make untruth look so attractive.

Mr. Pink has made many more unscriptural statements in his booklet, *The Doctrine of Election,* and not a few of these expose his ignorance of the Pauline commission. However, I will close here so as not to belabor points already brought out.

God's best always and, again, I know you understand that in writing this I do not have personalities in view, neither that of Mr. Pink or any other person.

> Affectionately in Christ,
>
> Signed / C. R. Stam

A Personal Letter On the Writings of Arthur W. Pink

FURTHER CONSIDERATION

**Christ's Death for All the
Only Legitimate Basis for the
Gospel of the Grace of God**

That the saved are God's elect, "chosen in Christ before the foundation of the world," we do not deny. Rather we believe and rejoice in this blessed truth.

That Christ, in His death, paid the penalty for the sins of the elect *alone* we *DO DENY.*

That "the world" for whom Christ died is only "the world of the elect" we MOST EMPHATICALLY DENY.

Many Scripture passages unite to declare that salvation is *the gift of God,* to be received *by faith,* but how can I accept in faith a gift which is in no way intended for me? How can salvation even be validly offered to those for whom no such provision was made?

Suppose a wealthy man makes a will, leaving great riches to certain unknown persons, described only as "the elect." The *testator* has certain particular individuals in mind but does not identify them in any way. After the testator dies *how can any living person possibly claim any portion of his will or inherit any of the riches described therein?* Such a will would, on its face, be null and void since no one could possibly know who was included in it.

Thus, we submit, if the riches of grace that Christ purchased at Calvary were purchased only for an *unidentified* few, *none* can legitimately accept these riches *by faith,* for how can anyone know that he belongs to the unidentified few, the elect, known to God alone?

Some may say, as *we* do: "Ask Him to save you, and see if He will not do so." But this is not the point of our argument. The point is: How can one *accept in faith* that which God has not specifically offered *to him?* And how can we legitimately offer salvation to all if Christ died only for "the elect"?

IF CHRIST DID NOT DIE FOR ALL
HOW DO YOU KNOW
HE DIED FOR *YOU?*

In the following discussion, (**A**) believes that Christ died *only* for the elect; (**B**) believes He died for all men.

A. I am so glad I can say that Christ died for *ME;* not just for everybody, but for *ME.*

B. But how do you *KNOW* He died for you if He did not die for everybody?

A. Because I trust in Him as my Savior and John 3:36 says: "He that believeth on the Son hath everlasting life."

B. Ah, but *how* is He your Savior? Why believe on *Him* to be saved; why not Bhudda?

A. Because Christ, not Bhudda, died for my sins.

B. But how do you know He died for *YOUR* sins? Did He *say* this? You say He died only for the elect and these are only a small minority of mankind, known to God alone.

A. I believe the Holy Spirit wrought faith in my heart; that He caused me to believe.

B. But my point is: How can you *believe* what God *has not said?* If Christ died

ELECTION

only for the elect, and He did not say that you are one of the elect, how can you believe He died for *you?* How can you believe *what He did not say?*

A. Well, He didn't say He died for *you,* either.

B. Yes He did. He says He "gave Himself a ransom for all" (I Tim. 2:6), and "tasted death for every man" (Heb. 2:9), and surely that includes me.

A. But how do you account for the fact that His Spirit bears witness with my spirit that I am a child of God? (Rom. 8:16).

B. According to *your belief* this could be nothing more than *supportive* evidence *IF* it is first established that you are one of the elect. "The heart is deceitful above all things," so that we cannot establish our salvation on human experience.

But if Christ died only for the elect (a small minority of mankind), and He didn't *say* He died for *you,* then you are *NOT* basing your faith for salvation on the *Word* of God, are you?

A. Well. . . . (Is there any valid answer to this question except "No"?)

CHRIST DIED FOR ME

Every believer in Christ rejoices, or should rejoice, with Paul in the blessed fact that *"He loved me, and gave Himself for me"* (Gal. 2:20). Some, to make this truth very personal, have substituted their own names for the twice-repeated "me" in this passage of Scripture.

This joy can be turned into *pure selfishness,* however, if we do not also believe, and proclaim from the housetops that "by the grace of God" our Lord *"tasted death for every man"* (Heb. 2:9). Mark well, the apostle does not use the word "world" here, but the term *"every man."* What great love in His heart, then, for every individual sinner! This agrees with the *"so loved the world"* of John 3:16.

Indeed, it is the rejection of this offer of love that places upon *every individual unbeliever* the condemnation due him.

This is why the passage in John 3 above, goes on to say:

"He that believeth on Him is not condemned, but he that believeth not is condemned already,

BECAUSE HE HATH NOT BELIEVED in the name of the only begotten Son of God" (John 3:18).

And this is why II Thes. 2:7-12 declares that God will give the unbelieving world up to Antichrist, "the man of sin,"

". . . BECAUSE THEY RECEIVED NOT THE LOVE OF THE TRUTH, THAT THEY MIGHT BE SAVED.

"And FOR THIS CAUSE God shall send them strong delusion, that they should believe a lie:

"THAT THEY ALL MIGHT BE DAMNED WHO BELIEVED NOT THE TRUTH, BUT HAD PLEASURE IN UNRIGHTEOUSNESS."

So, unsaved friend, we beg you to reconsider the glad news that also places upon you a grave responsibility:

CHRIST DIED FOR YOU

Chapter VI

Can "All Men" Mean All *Kinds* of Men?
(A Study of I Timothy 2:1-7)

I Timothy 2, Verses 1-7, are manifestly important to us as believers living under "the dispensation of the grace of God," because they deal with a basic aspect of the particular message committed to the Apostle Paul for those of this dispensation. This is clearly stated in Verse 7.

Ver. 4 states plainly that God *"will have all men to be saved, and to come unto the knowledge of the truth."* This is His desire.[1] Vers. 5,6 state further that "there is one Mediator between God and *men,* "not *some* men," but *"men."* Finally, Ver. 6 states that Christ "gave Himself a ransom for *all."*

Some have placed a question mark behind these clear statements of Scripture because in Ver. 1 Paul also states that "supplications, prayers, interces-

---

1. The Greek *thrlo* in I Tim. 2:4 does not refer to God's *purpose* but to His *desire.* It is a much softer word than *bow lemen.* In I Tim. 2:4 *"will"* signifies the gracious desire of God for all men to be saved. *(Expository Dictionary of New Testament Words* by W. E. Vine.)

sions, and giving of thanks [should] be made for all men." Since, they argue, we cannot give thanks for all men, the "all" and the "all men" throughout the passage must mean all *kinds* of men: all, *without distinction* rather than all, *without exception.*

We propose to prove in this chapter that the "all" and the "all men" in this passage mean all *without exception;* that they *cannot* mean all without distinction.

1. The very use of the phrase "all, without distinction," is a *mis*use of the English language. Our *Webster's Unabridged Dictionary* does not include this definition for the word "all." "All men" mean all men, not some men, and if we mean all *kinds* of men, without *distinction,* we should state this or indicate it clearly in the context so that the "all" will correctly apply to the kinds of men rather than to the men.

2. The passages does not say that God would have all kinds of men to be saved or that Christ gave Himself a ransom for all kinds of men. Is God so impoverished in language that He could not have said

Can "All Men" Mean All Kinds of Men?

that He loves all kinds of men if He meant this, or that He could not at least have indicated it clearly if this was His meaning?

3. If we stop and think for a moment it becomes clear that "all, without exception" includes "all, without distinction," while the reverse is obviously not the case: all, without distinction, does not include all, without exception.

Thus, if I Tim. 2:1 refers to all kinds of men, it cannot mean all men, while if it refers to all men it simply means that all should be included in our prayer interest: supplications, prayers and intercessions being made for some, and giving of thanks for others.

4. If Verse 1 means merely that we should *pray,* intercede, etc., for all *kinds* of men, for all *without distinction,* would it not also be clearly saying that we should give thanks for all kinds of men? Yet this is the very argument that Limited Redemptionists present against our insistence that "all men" means *all men!* (See again Paragraph 3 of this chapter). Thus the argument that God

here refers only to all, *without distinction,* crumbles at the very outset.

5. If Verse 1 refers merely to all kinds of men, would not God have said in Verse 2, "for kings and for slaves, for sinners and saints, for the educated and the illiterate," or something to this effect? But He does not say this. He says rather, "Pray for kings and for *all that are in authority.*" Here the all cannot refer to all without distinction, for He clearly speaks of *one kind* of person only: *"those who are in authority."* And why does He exhort us to pray for these? The answer is: "that we may lead a quiet and peaceable life . . . for this is good and acceptable in the sight of God . . . who will have all men to be saved." In other words, we should pray for kings and for those who are in authority because God would have the gospel to go forth under peaceful circumstances *since it is His desire that all should be saved.*

6. Paul's statement in I Timothy 2 does not stand alone. Heb. 2:9 declares that Christ "tasted death for *every man*" (How could this possibly mean all, with-

out distinction?), and John 3:16,17 clearly states that God loved "the world" into which Christ came, and which He did not wish to condemn. Therefore, to teach that John 3:16 refers only to "the world of the elect," is a perversion of plain Scripture.

Elsewhere we have listed numerous Scripture passages which all confirm the simple declaration of I Tim. 2:1-7: that God desires the salvation of all men and that Christ gave Himself a ransom for all.

7. If a man should read in the Scriptures that God loves all men and that Christ died for all men, would it even occur to him (apart from the defense of a theological doctrine) that God meant only all kinds of men, but did not include all? "All men" means all men, not all kinds of men, unless the word "kind" is used directly with the word "all," or there is in the context some clear statement or implication that would qualify the word "all."

8. JOHN CALVIN says, regarding this passage: "GOD HAS AT HEART THE

SALVATION OF ALL, BECAUSE HE INVITES ALL TO THE ACKNOWLEDGMENT OF THE TRUTH" *(Calvin's Commentaries,* at I Tim. 2:4. Emphasis ours).

The word "because," in Calvin's statement is most significant. Calvin shows, here, a keenness of insight that some of his followers lack at this point. He saw clearly that it would have been dishonest on the part of God to invite all to salvation if He did not desire the salvation of all. Indeed, Calvin emphasizes God's desire for the salvation of all in many of his comments on passages like the above.

Perhaps it would be well for our Limited Redemption brethren—and for us all—to put aside all preconceived notions and to read, simply read, I Tim. 2:4-7 with open heart and mind, as if we had never read it before.

LET'S THINK THIS THROUGH

(Please do not read this hurriedly. If you do not have time to read it thoughtfully now, please lay it aside until you can give it a thoughtful reading.)

Can "All Men" Mean All Kinds of Men?

First, let us read I Timothy 2:4-7 *just as it is.* Don't alter it. Don't add to it. Just *read* it—*thoughtfully.*

"[God our Savior] will have all men to be saved, and to come unto the knowledge of the truth.

"For there is one God, and one Mediator between God and men, the man Christ Jesus;

"Who gave Himself a ransom for all, to be testified in due time.

"Whereunto I am ordained a preacher, and an apostle, (I speak the truth in Christ, and lie not;) a teacher of the Gentiles in faith and verity."

Here we are told that it is God's desire that "all men" should be saved, and that Christ gave Himself a ransom for "all." This is also what the *Received Greek Text* says.

If God had meant merely that He would have all *kinds* of men to be saved ("all, without distinction") He could have said this, couldn't He? *But He didn't.* He said *"all men."* If the 47 translators of the *Authorized Version,* all great Greek scholars, had thought that God *meant* to say that He would have all *kinds* of men to be saved, they could have translated it this way, couldn't they? *But they didn't.*

ELECTION

They understood God to mean that He would have (i.e., He *desired*) "ALL MEN" to be saved.

If God had meant merely that Christ gave Himself a ransom for all *kinds* of people, he could have said so, couldn't He? *But He didn't.* He said that Christ "gave Himself a ransom *for all.*" If the 47 translators of the *Authorized Version* had believed that God *meant* that Christ gave Himself a ransom for all *kinds* of people, they could have translated His words so, couldn't they? *But they didn't.* They clearly believed that God meant just what He said, that Christ "gave Himself a ransom *FOR ALL.*"

Is it argued that the *Authorized* translators were biased? Then listen to this: Of the 34 different translations this writer has in his library, NOT ONE upholds the "all *kinds*" ("all without distinction") theory. EVERY SINGLE ONE says that God would have "all men" to be saved and that Christ gave Himself a ransom "for *all.*"

It is indeed wonderful good news that God desires all men to be saved and that

Can "All Men" Mean All Kinds of Men?

Christ gave Himself a ransom for all. But notice that this "gospel of the grace of God" had not always been proclaimed. Paul states in Verses 6 and 7 that Christ "gave Himself a ransom for all, TO BE TESTIFIED IN DUE TIME."

"WHEREUNTO I AM ORDAINED A PREACHER, AND AN APOSTLE, (I SPEAK THE TRUTH IN CHRIST, AND LIE NOT;) A TEACHER OF THE GENTILES IN FAITH AND VERITY."

This good news, then, is a message of grace first committed to the Apostle Paul—and so to us. If we change its wording to mean merely that God would have all *kinds* of men to be saved, and that Christ died only for all *kinds* of men, i.e., that God loves, and Christ died for, only the elect, are we not departing from the great Pauline revelation which God has entrusted to us to proclaim to others?

Believe in election—you should, for it is a truth clearly proclaimed in the Word of God. But never forget that God elected "according to His foreknowledge," not because He arbitrarily loved some and hated others.

How can it be that God loved some and hated others, much less because He hated the vast majority of mankind, when it was to the *unregenerate* Corinthians that Paul proclaimed the good news: *"Christ died for our sins."* Read I Corinthians 15:1-3 carefully.

A FURTHER THOUGHT FOR CONSIDERATION

If some preacher, unknown to you, were to say: "I believe that all men will be saved," would you not immediately conclude that he was a Universalist?

Suppose further that, approaching him about this, he should say: "I am not a Universalist. I mean that all *kinds* of men will be saved." Would you not rightly respond: *"Why didn't you say so?"*

Would this not apply as legitimately to God's Word in I Timothy 2:4-7—Greek or English?

Five additional terms confirm the above.

In John 3:16,17 we read that "God . . . loved THE WORLD," *the world into which* He "sent His son." How could this possibly refer to the elect alone?

I John 2:2 states that Christ is "the propitiation (satisfaction) not for our sins only, but also for the sins of THE

WHOLE WORLD." How could this possibly include the elect alone?

In Hebrews 2:9 we read that "by the grace of God" our Lord "tasted death for EVERY MAN." How could this possibly include the elect alone?

In II Peter 3:9 God says that He is "not willing that ANY should perish, [How could this possibly include the elect alone?] but that ALL should come to repentance."

There you have it: "THE WORLD," "THE WHOLE WORLD," "EVERY," "ANY," "ALL."

To seek to explain *any* of these away would surely be a sin against God—but *all five of them?!*

Chapter VII

All This to Maintain a Position

We appreciate the desire of our "Limited Redemption" brethren to prove from the Scriptures that true believers (who comprise a very small minority of mankind) are saved by *the sovereign grace of God.* We heartily agree with them in this.

However, in their belief that God does not *love* all men and that Christ did not *die for* all men, they fail to appreciate another aspect of grace, i.e., that *"the grace of God, and the gift by grace . . . hath abounded to many* [Gr. *the* many]."

To maintain their doctrine of *limited love* and *limited redemption* they must alter some of the most precious passages of Scripture as, e.g., the following:

John 3:16: The word "world" here does not mean the *world,* they say, but only the world of the elect.

I John 2:2: "The whole world," in this passage, does not mean *the whole world.*

It means *all the elect,* or possibly elect Gentiles.

II Cor. 5:15: This passage does not really mean that our Lord *"died for all,"* but only for all the elect, or possibly for all *kinds* of people.

I Tim. 2:4-6: This does not really mean that God desires *"all men* to be saved," or that Christ "gave Himself a ransom for *all."* It refers either to all *elect* men, or all *kinds* of men.

Heb. 2:9: This statement does not mean that our Lord "tasted death for *every man."* Since the actual word *"man"* does not appear in the original, it probably means every cause, or every reason: anything but "every man"! But the Greeks used the term "every" for *every man,* just as we use the word "all" for *all men!*

II Pet. 3:9: This passage does not mean that God does not desire "that *any* should perish," or that He would have *all* to "come to repentance." It means that He does not will that any of *the elect* should perish but that all of *them* should come to repentance.

In other words, none of the above passages mean *what they say*. *"The world"* doesn't mean the world, *"the whole world"* doesn't mean the whole world, "all" doesn't mean all, "all men" doesn't mean all men, "any" and "all" don't really mean that, "every man" doesn't mean every man (though this *is* the sense in the Greek). *None* of these precious Bible verses mean what they say; they all mean something else.

Strangely, though, the meanings of all these passages are altered to maintain *one unscriptural doctrine:* the teaching that God does *not* love all men and that Christ did *not* die for all.

Yet we read in II Pet. 2:1 that Christ died even for false teachers, doomed to destruction:

"**. . . there shall be FALSE TEACHERS among you, who privily shall bring in damnable heresies, EVEN DENYING THE LORD THAT BOUGHT THEM, and bring upon themselves swift destruction.**"

Shall we not then believe with all our hearts, and thank God with all our hearts, for the above declarations of grace, that "God so loved *the world,*" that Christ's death is the payment, not only for *our* sins but *also* for those of *"the whole world,"* that He "died *for all,*" and "would have *all men* to be saved," having given Himself "a ransom *for all,*" tasting death "for *every man,*" because it is not His will "that *any* should perish, but that *all* should come to repentance"? What a message we have! What grace that has sent us to declare to the king on his throne, or the drunkard in the gutter: *"Your sins have been paid for. Believe and be saved!"*

Chapter VIII

Twenty Problems for Limited Redemptionists to Solve

1. In John 8:12 and 9:5 Christ called Himself "the Light of the world." Limited Redemptionists say that He meant that He was the light of "the world of the elect." But in Matthew 5:14, Christ also calls His disciples "the light of the world." Did He mean that they should be *lights to the elect alone?* How would they know whom the elect were?

2. The term "world" is often clearly used in Scripture to include the lost, but *is it ever clearly used to include only the elect?*

3. In I John 2:2 we read that Christ gave Himself as a satisfaction for the sins of "the whole world." Our Limited Redemptionist friends argue that this means the whole world of the elect. But in I John 5:19 the same phrase is used. Here we read that *"the whole world* lieth

*Twenty Problems
for Limited Redemptionists to Solve*

in wickedness [or, the wicked one]." Yet here they assure us that the same phrase refers to all the *unsaved* in this world system!

---

4. When our Lord said: "I pray not for the world" (John 17:9), could He have meant that He did not *also* pray for the world, when we find Him doing just this in Verse 21, where He prays that His own might be one: "that the world may believe that Thou has sent Me"? The phrase: "I pray not for the world," will be easily understood if we simply bring the English up to date and render it: "I am not praying for the world." At that particular moment He was praying for His own, not for the world.

---

5. In arguing that all for whom Christ died will be saved, our Limited Redemption friends frequently use the phrase: "the cross saves," but this is hardly a legitimate argument for Limited Redemption. We believe as thoroughly as they that the cross saves—in the same sense in which a remedy cures.

6. Many Limited Redemptionists teach that whatever God desires He brings to pass. But did He not make it very clear to our first parents that He did not wish them to eat of the fruit of the tree of the knowledge of good and evil, yet they *did* eat of it. Was He frustrated? Or, did He wish them to eat of it though He commanded them not to?

7. From II Cor. 5:13,14 we learn that "the love of Christ" constrained Paul to preach the gospel. Did Paul love only the elect?

8. To offer salvation to a public audience simply because the value of Christ's death was infinite, is not legitimate. How can the infinite worth of His death, by itself, afford ground for offering salvation to all men?

9. The Limited Redemptionists say that since faith pleases God and only the regenerate can please God, therefore only the regenerate can believe. They base this on Hebrews 11:6 and John 6:29. However in this they make faith some sort of good work which God will accept

*Twenty Problems
for Limited Redemptionists to Solve*

from the sinner. Yet in Paul's epistles he constantly sets faith over against works; they are placed in juxtaposition to each other, e.g., "by grace are ye saved, through faith . . . NOT of works. . . ."

---

10. If faith was purchased by Christ only for the benefit of the elect, as Limited Redemptionists teach, it is the only benefit not received through believing, for obviously men do not receive *faith* by *believing!* Faith is believing.

---

11. Our Lord's statement that "no man can come unto Me, except the Father draw him," in no way implies that the drawing of the Father cannot be resisted. We know that it is resisted by some. It is dangerous to read into the Scriptures more than they actually say. The inability of the non-elect to trust Christ is a completely criminal inability, one for which they themselves are held responsible.

---

12. In Genesis 37:4 we are told that Joseph's brethren "could not speak peaceably unto him" because they hated him. This inability to speak peaceably to Joseph was, however, not an inescapable

necessity to them; it was *criminal* inability. They did not have to hate Joseph.

---

13. Hebrews 2:3 declares: "How shall we escape if we neglect so great salvation?" Does this passage not clearly imply that salvation through Christ was being offered to some who, if they neglected it, would suffer eternal damnation? Can it be that salvation *had not been provided* for those who neglected to appropriate it?

---

14. Can there be any doubt that in Scripture the sinner is consistently addressed as responsible to take action on the promises, commandments and offers made to him by God? The very fact that the glorified Lord sent Paul—and us—to preach the gospel of the grace of God to all men, without imposing any limitation, indicates that there must have been no limitation to His redeeming sacrifice; that Christ died for all.

---

15. When speaking of the death of Christ the Scriptures often make use of

general terms, extending it to all, while in mentioning predestination they always use *distinctive* terms, limiting it to the few. How can this be if Christ died only for the elect?

---

16. Would God tell us: "Love your enemies," and then hate His own enemies? Is it not God-like to love our enemies?

---

17. God's love as shown to man in nature and providence indicates that God "would have all men to be saved" (I Tim. 2:4). It indicates that while He permits many to perish, this is not His desire for them.

---

18. Is it not a misrepresentation of God's love and grace to deny that God has provided salvation for all men, in the face of plain Scriptures that declare this to be true?

---

19. If the Limited Redemptionists are right, the general invitations of the Bible, including the very last one in Rev. 22:17, are without legitimate basis. Indeed, in that case they are a mockery, *offering to*

non-elect sinners that which has not been provided for them.

---

20. If Christ did not die for all, is there really any gospel, any good news, for the non-elect?

It has been rightly said that "it is possible to hold a few texts so near to one's eyes that they hide the rest of the Bible."

APPENDIX

A Touching Letter from a Reader

The writer of the letter below, along with his family, came from the same background as the author, so we well understand the anguish of heart that can come from the doctrine that God does not love, and that Christ did not die for all men. This anguish is surely not unfounded.

This letter was first published in pamphlet form, with the writer's permission. Now we include it in this volume.

March 11, 1974

Dear Pastor Stam:

Greetings in the wonderful name of Christ. We haven't forgotten you, although much, so much, has transpired since we last corresponded, that we just have not had time to inform you until now. Here is the Good News!

After years of struggle and much confusion (on our part) the Lord has proven faithful to His Word . . . in delivering the souls of my household. He saved me 22 years ago this past January 12th. On Sunday, January 27th of this year, He saved our youngest first (my daughter). Then on Tuesday night, February 12th, He saved my son. The following Sunday afternoon, February 17th, He displayed His marvelous grace again in the salvation of my dear wife . . . who had been deceived by Calvinistic doctrines and the wiles of the Devil for so great a time. Perhaps the Calvinistic doctrines were all right in themselves, but her understanding of them left her helpless and in despair of ever being saved.

Pastor Stam, you have no idea of the joy we have experienced this past month. God is able to do exceeding abundantly above whatever we ask or think. And for good measure, the Lord also saved my son's fiance, Thursday, February 21st, while she was at work. The only Scripture she knew and the Lord used, was John 3:16. They are planning to get married May 11th of this year.

Now for more facts. We received a copy of an article printed by you entitled "The Doctrine of Limited Redemption—Is It

Appendix

Scriptural." God used this article in loosing my lost loved ones from the snare of the Devil. In fact, the very day my son was saved he was discussing this very article which seemingly held out hope for him, that he was included in Christ's vicarious sacrifice, and became determined to come to Christ by faith through the Word, guided by the Holy Spirit. We will never be able to thank you enough. The truth contained in this article unlocked the door of salvation and the flood gates of Grace. May we have 3 more [copies] of the same article?

We are enclosing a gift of $30.00. If you like, you may apply it to your radio account, as we listen to you every Sunday morning. May this letter find you in good health, enjoying God's richest blessings, which I know is the fruit of your labors for our Lord.

With Christian love,

Signed: (name withheld)

Dr. Arno C. Gaebelein's View of Arthur. W. Pink's Book the Sovereignty of God

Dr. Arno C. Gaebelein was once asked to comment on "The Sovereignty of God," Arthur W. Pink's extreme book on Election. Said Dr. Gaebelein:

"Mr. Pink used to be a contributor to our magazine. His articles on "Gleanings in Genesis" are good, and we had them printed in book form. But when he began to teach his frightful doctrines, which make the God of Love a monster, we broke off fellowship with him. . . . The book you have read is totally unscriptural. It is akin to blasphemy. It represents God as a Being of injustice, and maligns His holy character. The book denies that our blessed Lord died for the ungodly. According to Pink's perversions He died only for the elect. . . . You are not the only one who has been led into darkness by this book. Whoever the publisher is, and whoever stands behind the circulation of such a monstrous thing has a grave responsibility. It is just the kind of teaching that makes atheists."

THE BEREAN BIBLE SOCIETY

• For over 50 years the *Berean Bible Society* has been "An Organization for the Promotion of Bible Study." Standing firm on the fundamentals of the Christian faith, it employs many means to interest people in the study of the Scriptures, among them the following:

• BBS arranges *Bible Conferences* for the study of the Word. Its President, Paul Sadler, has spoken at many such conferences throughout the United States and Canada.

• The Society publishes the *Berean Searchlight,* a Bible study magazine edited by Pastor Sadler, and sent free of charge to readers in every state in the Union and more than 60 foreign countries.

• *"Two Minutes With the Bible,"* a weekly newspaper column featured in hundreds of newspapers across the country, is another means BBS uses to reach the masses with the Word. This column now has a weekly readership running into the millions.

• *Tape recorded messages* are provided free of charge through our free lending library and for use in Bible classes. Some taped messages are offered for sale at modest prices.

• BBS has been proclaiming the message of grace for many years through *radio broadcasts* in many parts of the country.

• Finally, BBS offers *Daily Bible Lessons by Telephone* as a special service to Chicagoland. The number: (708) 453-1010.

• These growing ministries are carried on by the voluntary contributions of believers who desire to see others reached with the truths that have brought so much light and blessing to their own lives.

THE BEREAN BIBLE SOCIETY
7609 West Belmont Avenue   Chicago, Illinois 60635

OTHER BOOKS BY THE SAME AUTHOR

Things That Differ (w/Bible Index)
Rightly Dividing the Word of Truth

The Controversy (w/Bible Index)
A 35-year Test of Pauline Truth

Acts Dispensationally Considered (4 Volumes)
w/Bible Study Chart and Maps of Paul's Journeys

The Sermon On the Mount
And the Gospel of the Grace of God

The Twofold Purpose of God
Prophecy and the Mystery

Moses and Paul
The Dispensers of Law and Grace

Our Great Commission
What Is It?

True Spirituality
The Secret of a Blessed Christian Life

Satan In Derision
The Heart of the Mystery

Two Minutes with the Bible
A Daily Bible Study Devotional

Man, His Nature and Destiny (w/Bible Index)

Baptism and the Bible

The Lord's Supper and the Bible

Commentary on the Epistle to the Romans

Commentary on First Corinthians

Commentary on the Thessalonian Epistles

Commentary on the Pastoral Epistles

The Present Peril
The New Evangelicalism

No Other Doctrine

Paul His Apostleship and Message

Suggestions For Young Pastors

The Author's Choice
Of His Own Writings

BEREAN BIBLE SOCIETY
7609 W. Belmont Ave., Chicago, IL 60635

Things That Differ

THE FUNDAMENTALS OF DISPENSATIONALISM

By CORNELIUS R. STAM

A Comprehensive Study of Dispensational Truth

Contains: Nearly 300 pages, 15 chapters, Bible Index, 8 Bible Study charts and a quiz at the close of each chapter.

- Demonstrates how the dispensational method of Bible Study is the method God approves, and the only one by which the Bible makes sense.

- Shows the perfect harmony between the changeless principles of God and His changing dispensations.

- Points out the distinctions between prophecy and the mystery, the kingdom of heaven and the Body of Christ, the ministries of Peter and Paul, the Rapture of believers and the revelation of Christ, the various gospels, etc.

- Establishes which is our "great commission," deals with miraculous signs and water baptism, answers extreme dispensationalists and explains the dispensational position of the Lord's Supper.

- *The Fundamentals of Dispensationalism* provides Bible lovers with many hours of delightful Bible study and supplies pastors, Sunday School teachers, Christian workers with ideas and subjects for hundreds of illuminating Bible messages.

Our Best Seller *By far!*

If this book has proved a blessing to you, please help us get it out to others.

Do you receive our monthly Bible study magazine, THE BEREAN SEARCHLIGHT? It is sent free of charge to any who request it.

A COMPLETE PRICE LIST
. . . is available free of charge. Address your request to:

BEREAN BIBLE SOCIETY
7609 W. Belmont Ave., Chicago, IL 60635

NOTES

NOTES

NOTES

NOTES

NOTES

NOTES

NOTES

NOTES

NOTES

NOTES

NOTES

NOTES